PRESENTS

Achieve Your Goals!
Workshop

The Quest Master® Guide to Unleashing Your Success

"Achieve Your Goals" is a production of Artimaginaton, Inc. and is the companion book for Quest Master® achievement tools. This is not a user manual for Quest Master®. This book "Achieve Your Goals" is an inspirational guide to help you achieve your goals (whether or not you own Quest Master®, although we believe you will find that owning Quest Master is an invaluable and inexpensive tool to achieving success).

You can learn more about Quest Master® achievement tools at **www.Quest.bz**

We hope that you enjoy and are inspired by this book.

We look forward to hearing your thoughts.

To contact the Quest Master® team:

Email: Service@Quest.bz
Website: www.Quest.bz

Quest Master is a federally registered trademark of Artimagination, Inc. Artwork and text Copyright © 2015 M. Nicole van Dam used under license by Artimagination, Inc. All Rights Reserved. No part of this book may be used or reproduced in any manner whatsoever without the express written permission of Artimagination, Inc. and M. Nicole van Dam.

Table of Contents

Getting Started	Page 4
Know Thyself	Page 5
Do for Thyself	Page 46
Accountability for Your Dreams	Page 52
Inspiration	Page 54
Journaling Pages	Page 56
About Quest Master®	Page 98
Quest Master® for Business	Page 100

Success is something we design for ourselves

Getting Started

Exploring the Successful You

Use this book to get started on a daring adventure... exploring the successful and creative side of YOU. So many people talk themselves out of pursuing their dreams. Learn hands on techniques for releasing the inhibitions and combating the negative self-talk that can stifle achievement. We hope you join us for this unique innovative journey, filled with smiles, insights and inspiration.

Please have a pen or pencil handy when you read this book – this book will ask you to answer some questions. The act of answering those questions will help clarify not only next steps to achieving your dreams, but also reveal how you approach life and pre-conceptions that might be holding you back. Honestly and thoughtfully answering these questions will help you define and address those things that hold you back. You might even find yourself smiling as you acknowledge some of the foibles that have been hurdles in the past. We also recommend that you purchase Quest Master® achievement tools as a way to track your progress in achieving your goals.

Achieving your goals is what the Quest Master® achievement app is all about. You can either use Quest Master® with this book as noted below in the following steps, or you can entirely complete the process in this book without Quest Master.

Of course, we highly recommend Quest Master! What makes the Quest Master® Achievement software/cell phone app unique and helpful is that Quest Master® works for any type of goal, it allows you to track your progress towards each goal easily, and it allows you to input and view income, expenses, photos, audio, video, notes, contacts, and events both by goal and by type. In other words, at a glance you can see all the income, expenses, photos, audio, video, notes, contacts, and events associated with a particular goal of yours, or you can see all your notes together, all your income items together, etc.

Quest Master® is ideal for the entrepreneur, start-up business owner, artist, software programmer, photographer, writer, chef/recipe collector, hobbyist, or anyone seeking to achieve a dream. The patent pending Quest Master® software is provided to you by the Quest

Master team at Artimagination, Inc. The Quest Master team actually used a beta version of the Quest Master® achievement app to build Quest Master!

Please visit www.Quest.bz to learn more or to find where to purchase Quest Master.

KNOW THYSELF

Clarifying Your Thoughts

Before you can get to where you want to be, you need to clarify your thoughts just a bit. This is an ongoing process, not something you set in stone and put away and decide now you know yourself forever.

On the pages that follow, you will be asked a few questions that are designed to help you learn about you. Please keep in mind that what you say now may not be true for tomorrow or yesterday or next year – that's OK – you don't need to provide a forever answer. You just need to write what is true for right now.

The first step to knowing yourself is to ask yourself how you respond when faced with a new, somewhat intimidating challenge. Write down on the following pages what you can remember telling yourself in the past to give yourself confidence:

_____

_____

_____

_____

SUCCESS IS SOMETHING WE DESIGN FOR OURSELVES

1. Introducing the "Itty Bitty Shitty Committee"

Do you ever hear any naysayers in your head? Do you, like so many people, have an inner critical voice or voices that tell you negative things about your plans or dreams or capabilities? I call this negative inner voice – in my case a whole committee chimes in sometime - the "itty bitty shitty committee." Write below what you hear your negative inner voice(s) say when you think about achieving your dreams or trying something new:

_____

_____

_____

_____

SUCCESS IS SOMETHING WE DESIGN FOR OURSELVES

SUCCESS IS SOMETHING WE DESIGN FOR OURSELVES

These negative voices can be paralyzing – our negative inner voices can prevent us from even trying to achieve our goals. Inner negative voices can also be cannibalistic to your creative solution-making process.

The best way to combat the detrimental impact of these negative voices is to get to know them – to analyze these negative voices. For example, when you have to face a difficult challenge or wish to try something new, how many of these naysayers do you think there are? For some it's one voice, for others it's a whole committee.

As I said earlier, I call this negative committee the "itty bitty shitty committee," because I found it was helpful to give a name that made me smile to these inner negative voices. Being able to smile at these negative inner voices helps me minimize the detrimental impact my inner negative self-talk could have on my outlook and capabilities.   Give your negative inner voice(s) a name now:

_____

SUCCESS IS SOMETHING WE DESIGN FOR OURSELVES

Now let's poke some fun at our itty bitty shitty committee:

Using stick figure type circles as faces, draw the expressions that you can imagine on your itty bitty shitty committee faces:

Remember these funny pictures that you drew above the next time any member of your itty bitty shitty committee makes an appearance! It will help you put your itty bitty shitty committee members in their place!

There can be a lot of deep psychology behind the itty bitty shitty committee. For example, the voices of the itty bitty shitty committee can be what was drilled into you in the past by family or school or past criticism from a powerful figure in your life, or from books or movies that impressed you. The negative voices can also be a reflection of a fear of failure.

A point to keep in mind, though, is that these inner voices are no more real than imagining wild success beyond your dreams – the negative voices reflect one possible outcome perhaps, but not EVERY possible outcome.

2. Fear of Failure

Many of us have heard of people not doing, not trying, because they have a fear of failure. What is the fear of failure? Some people say the fear of failure is things like:
- Being laughed at
- Tripping up in front of everybody
- Being pitied
- Being noticed at a time when you look less than perfect
- Who are you to think your dreams are worthy of seeing the light of day, of taking up anybody's time.
- Whole itty bitty shitty committee out there saying don't do this, you're going to make an ass of yourself, I told you this wouldn't work, you're such an idiot and if you do this the whole world will know it.

Write down below how you define failure:

_____

_____

_____

SUCCESS IS SOMETHING WE DESIGN FOR OURSELVES

SUCCESS IS SOMETHING WE DESIGN FOR OURSELVES

_____

_____

_____

_____

_____

_____

_____

One of the biggest inhibitors to striving for success and achieving your goals is that the very act of trying does reveal you, makes you vulnerable, puts you in a position where you can be judged...we all have heard the old saying – "Don't give up your day job."

Let's face it, it takes a bit of audacity, especially if we look around us and say, "I'm no better than the other guys, why would success happen for me?"

In fact, some of the most intimidating failure feelings can come when we look at the other guy.

Our inner voices start saying things like "She does this better than I can." -But that's ridiculously irrelevant isn't it? Her efforts are hers in response to her dreams, and my efforts are my efforts to achieve my dream. She isn't working for my dream, is she? If I want *my* dream, I need to do that work myself. It's not like only one person on the planet gets to achieve their goals! Two different people can each achieve their own goals, can't they?

Now there are good reasons to look at what others are doing.

For example, if I learn from or am inspired by another's efforts that's great!

However, the minute – the second – that I start thinking that I'm worth less because my abilities or results aren't as good or perfect as someone else's abilities or results, then that's BAD thinking, and that's got to be nipped in the bud.

In other words, you're playing unhealthy mind games with yourself if you use the other guy's success as an excuse to discourage your own efforts.

Ok, so when you think of failure, that's an emotionally charged word, for some a scary word. Sketch IN PENCIL below whatever shapes (and color in whatever shades) that come to mind when you think of failure:

Now ERASE part of what you drew above. Feel the POWER – you just ERASED failure!
Remember that – you have the power to visualize failure AND you have the power to erase

SUCCESS IS SOMETHING WE DESIGN FOR OURSELVES

your fear of failure. You have control over failure and what it means. You can erase it, you can learn from it! Failure doesn't erase you or who you are, failure doesn't control you – you're in control of how you treat failure!

3. There is only ONE Measuring Stick that Matters – and it's YOURS!

The only measurement stick that counts when judging success verses failure is you judging yourself against your unique capabilities and circumstances, just as I must judge myself against my unique capabilities and circumstances.

In other words, you should never judge your results against my results, or my results against your results. That's an exercise that leads nowhere good for either of us.

Why?

Let's face it, we're all born with different packages. Some of us are tall, some are super smart, some are naturally skilled at fixing things, some come with a great checkbook, some have charisma, etc. If in some things I am capable of more than others, then I should be grateful for my good fortune, but that God given capability doesn't make me superior, because in other things I know I've got work to do. For example, some people are naturally thin, like my husband's family, whereas for me my natural weight setpoint might be 10,000 pounds, it's a constant struggle. However, I'm a super speedy self-learner, and not everyone has that. I am more proud of the pounds I have lost and kept off, than of learning quickly, because one was the result of a struggle, the other was the result of a God given gift.

It is important to acknowledge and celebrate those things you're good at or naturally blessed with. Please write down those things you think you're good at or naturally blessed with, and don't be shy to say it:

_____

_____

SUCCESS IS SOMETHING WE DESIGN FOR OURSELVES

_____

_____

_____

_____

_____

_____

_____

The point is, comparing your abilities to what another person can do in order to judge yourself a failure makes no sense. In fact, it probably makes as much sense as saying someone else's dog barks louder than your dog, so you must be a failure! It's absolutely irrelevant!

In other words, the real issue is not what the results of these comparisons are, but why you made the comparison in the first place.

Comparing yourself to others in a way that makes you feel bad might be a sneeze of negativity or self-destructive behavior, a tendency to get yourself down on yourself.

SUCCESS IS SOMETHING WE DESIGN FOR OURSELVES

Once you are aware that you make self-destructive comparisons once in a while, then all you need to do is catch yourself the next time and smile. Think of the picture you drew of the itty bitty shitty committee and tell them to go home!

Keep in mind: It's healthy to look around, be inspired, see what's possible, learn, but if you find yourself scanning the horizon just to see how you measure up negatively, catch yourself and remind yourself that comparing yourself to someone else makes no more sense and simply irrelevant as a judgment tool. The only measuring stick that matters is your own.

4. ON TO THE GOOD STUFF – SUCCESS!

What is success? It will be different for every person. Some people say things like:

- Life fully lived
- Closure in knowing you gave your dreams a shot
- Success is in just the trying
- Being self-supportive and paying the bills
- Being a good father/mother/friend
- Having friends, mate, etc. – having true ones who love you warts and all

Write down below how you define success:

_____

_____

_____

_____

SUCCESS IS SOMETHING WE DESIGN FOR OURSELVES

SUCCESS IS SOMETHING WE DESIGN FOR OURSELVES

_____

_____

Sketch whatever shapes and tones come to mind when you think of success below:

Page 26
Achieve Your Goals

Now look back to what you drew when you thought of failure. Ask yourself, how do these things differ?

5. Sometimes bad events help us define "Success!"

A few years ago, right before a July 4 weekend, I received a questionable test result and spent the whole weekend worrying that I had cancer. I also spent the whole weekend looking at my life, and I discovered that I was so glad for each goal I had pursued. In fact, what I discovered was that I was happy for every goofy thing I ever tried. I was even happy for the mistakes I made but had a good time at. What I regretted was the time I spent NOT following my dreams and my heart.

I didn't spend one second regretting all the boneheaded things I did, and I never regretted leaving the bed unmade. Happily, the final test came out cancer-free, but the gift of that weekend was recognizing what it means to live life fully, and how important it is.

None of us have infinite lives. —And it doesn't need to be illness that causes us to redefine our lives – it can be loss of a loved one, losing a job, divorce – we lead many "lives" in this one physical life, and the only thing that is sure is CHANGE!

Edison tried 1800 times before he got the light bulb right!!!

Imagine failing at anything 1799 times and NOT giving up. How does one keep faith after 1000 failures?

How many things have you ever tried to do at least 1800 times?

Before you say, "I never tried and failed at anything so many times, I'd give up," remember learning to ride your bike! How about tennis or golf? Learning to play an instrument?

Success is something we design for ourselves

Write below some of the things that you've accomplished or learned over the years that initially took a lot of tries to learn how to do:

_____

_____

_____

_____

_____

_____

_____

_____

SUCCESS IS SOMETHING WE DESIGN FOR OURSELVES

_____

_____

_____

I suppose that if Edison had stopped at 1799 tries at the light bulb, some might have said Edison to be a failure that wasted a lot of money and time. But perhaps others would have applauded Edison, because Edison would have brought science to the point where the next guy could step in and get the bulb right, and Edison helped the world to dream about light at night.
In other words, success and failure aren't black and white concepts.

People who want to be negative will say anything negative just to be negative, and take any ammunition they can get, while people who are positive will find a positive slant.

It doesn't matter what *other people* say about your efforts – it matters that you tried and what you say in your soul.

Another thing the Edison example teaches is that the endpoints that we choose to determine success verses failure are artificial.

Yogi Berra said "we didn't lose the baseball game, we ran out of innings."

The point is, in real life, whether it's inventing the light bulb or achieving your goals, you are the one who decides how long the innings are and when the number of innings are over for you.

You determine the endpoints. You get to choose the measuring stick. Other people may try to set the measuring stick, but they are irrelevant, don't give other people that control. –And if you do decide to call the last inning, you can always feel successful by helping the next guy can step in.

List below all the people you know that tried to follow their dream, and if you feel happy for them that they tried, or if you think they are failures:

_____

_____

_____

_____

_____

_____

_____

_____

_____

SUCCESS IS SOMETHING WE DESIGN FOR OURSELVES

_____

_____

_____

_____

_____

_____

_____

_____

I am very proud when people add me to this list!

6. Putting Your Footprints on the Path to "Success"

Now that you've learned a bit about success and failure, let's get started on you achieving your dream – you are READY TO START!

Here is where the Quest Master® achievement tools can be very helpful. You can either use Quest Master® as noted below in the following steps, or you can complete this process in this book. To purchase the Quest Master® achievement tools please visit www.Quest.bz

What makes the Quest Master® Achievement software/cell phone app unique and helpful is that Quest Master® works for any type of goal, it allows you to track your progress towards each goal easily, and it allows you to input and view income, expenses, photos, audio, video, notes, contacts, and events both by goal and by type. In other words, at a glance you can see all the income, expenses, photos, audio, video, notes, contacts, and events associated with a particular goal of yours, or you can see all your notes together, all your income items together, etc.

Quest Master® is ideal for the entrepreneur, start-up business owner, artist, software programmer, photographer, writer, chef/recipe collector, hobbyist, or anyone seeking to achieve a dream. The patent pending Quest Master® software is provided to you by the Quest Master team at Artimagination, Inc. The Quest Master team actually used a beta version of the Quest Master® achievement app to build Quest Master!

Either input one to three "Quests" into Quest Master® OR write down below one to three things you would like to try to do right now, the dreams you wish you could achieve, if you could wave that magic wand and go for it:

_____

_____

_____

SUCCESS IS SOMETHING WE DESIGN FOR OURSELVES

_____

_____

Now write down below what's holding you back from trying:

_____

_____

_____

_____

_____

_____

SUCCESS IS SOMETHING WE DESIGN FOR OURSELVES

SUCCESS IS SOMETHING WE DESIGN FOR OURSELVES

BE AWARE OF SELF SABOTAGE

Some people, for reasons known better to an expert in psychology rather than myself, create obstacles to pursuing their goals.
Following are some common examples of the loads of excuses people make to not even take one tiny step towards achieving their goals – and if you recognize yourself in these, you are not alone. Simply take a deep breath and analyze your thinking again – make sure you are not being your own worst enemy:

- I have to have more money in the bank, I shouldn't even think of pursuing this at all, not even background research or prep work, until I have enough money in the bank to do the whole thing

- I need to wait until my kids are out of the house

- The house is too messy, I am too disorganized right now to start anything, I need to have less clutter in the house

- I need to wait til _____ happens - it's the "my life will really begin once _____ happens" syndrome. Well guess what, your life has already begun. Life doesn't wait for you to pay off your credit card or your kid graduates. Your life is NOW.

- My dream is just too big for a regular person without millionaire parents to do it.

- I need more education first

- I need to finish this other project first before I start what I really want to do (and guess what – that other project doesn't really ever get done!)

- I don't have the time to waste on stupid things like dreams that don't come true

SUCCESS IS SOMETHING WE DESIGN FOR OURSELVES

Write down below things you might be telling yourself to delay starting baby steps to your dream that might actually be self-sabotage:

___

___

___

___

___

___

___

___

SUCCESS IS SOMETHING WE DESIGN FOR OURSELVES

SUCCESS IS SOMETHING WE DESIGN FOR OURSELVES

_____

_____

_____

_____

_____

_____

It is VERY important to remember that you don't need to achieve your dream all at once!

You can make baby steps of progress towards your dream, one achievable step at a time. If you are using Quest Master® it is these achievable small baby steps that are referred to as TO-DOs.

If you ask some of your friends what their goals are, you might hear some of your friends choose goals that are so huge and unobtainable that it gives them an excuse to not try and achieve anything. If you catch yourself doing this, remind yourself of the following:

Complexity or cost of a goal is NOT a reason to avoid trying to take the tiniest of baby steps towards achieving your dream!

In actuality, no matter how big the dream, if it really is your dream, your passion, then you can always take baby steps.

You can start learning your industry, go to trade shows, do research on costs, start learning how to write a business plan and then write one, start creating a website for your business, learn how social media works, etc. —And these baby steps will benefit you no matter how your dream turns out! Mentors and people you meet, and what you learn, are all valuable assets you take with you into ANY future endeavor, so it is NOT a waste of time. ENJOY THE JOURNEY!

In addition to self-sabotage, sometimes people who love you (as well as those who don't) might throw up road blocks too.

While these negative outside influences can be totally unintentional on their part, destructive is destructive is destructive.

These people might truly worry about your future, or they might be projecting their own fears and doubts onto your dreams and onto you. Either way, the decision to pursue your dream is very personal to you.

Not everyone is fully aware of their own motives. Sometimes because a person passed up their own dream, they think everyone should make that choice.

I was lucky – my Father took chances and successfully lived his dream, and he with my Mother became my example. Nonetheless, my parents did say things about a career in art that still haunt me, that still are negative voices telling me I will fail eventually – and this is true even after both of them have told me how proud they are of my successes in art. Those negative words, especially from people who love you and whom you love, can be hard to overcome, but overcome them you must if you wish to pursue your dream.

In one line, avoiding sabotage means this:

You need to give yourself permission to try!

SUCCESS IS SOMETHING WE DESIGN FOR OURSELVES

Do for Thyself

7. Giving Yourself Permission

Either complete the following steps using Quest Master® OR use the space to write down below:

If you're like most people, you've spent the first part of your life doing what you thought you were supposed to do, and you may not have thought much about what you really wanted to do in this big, big world. Not surprisingly, you might not be 100% thrilled with where you wound up.

Either input one to ten "Quests" into Quest Master® OR write down below a bullet point list of what you WANT to do, not what you think you are supposed to do.

What you "SHOULD" do should not play into your list at all. For this exercise, liberate your mind from the word "should." This bullet point list is for you only, outside influences be damned!

7.1 Make Your Bullet Point List of What You Wish to Achieve

Either input one to ten "Quests" into Quest Master® OR write down below a list below of up to 10 bullet points of what you want to do, what you want for you. You won't need to share these bullet points, this is just for you:

_____

_____

SUCCESS IS SOMETHING WE DESIGN FOR OURSELVES

SUCCESS IS SOMETHING WE DESIGN FOR OURSELVES

SUCCESS IS SOMETHING WE DESIGN FOR OURSELVES

_____

_____

_____

Accountability for Your Dreams

Now you need to be ACCOUNTABLE for your own goals!

7.2   Keeping Journaling Pages

Either

     A. input into Quest Master® your baby steps (called "TO-DOs") and then document your progress (called "Accomplishments") into Quest Master® using notes, contacts, events, expenses, income items, photos, videos, audio notes,

     OR

     B. create hand written "Journaling Pages" using the Journaling Pages which follow.

Here are instructions:

1. <u>If you are using Quest Master®</u> you will already have input 1 – 10 Quests under Section 8.1 above. <u>If you are using the Journaling Pages that follow in this book</u>, then rewrite (in the spaces on the following pages) your Bullet Point List from section 8.1 above, *putting no more than One Bullet-point per four pages.*

2. <u>If you are using Quest Master®</u> input at least two TO-DOs for each Quest. Remember that a TO-DO is no more than a baby step that you could take on the journey to achieving your goal. <u>If you are using the Journaling Pages that follow</u>, then for each particular bullet point, write at least two things you can start doing now towards achieving that bullet point. EXAMPLES OF TO-DOs: If your Bullet Point (aka Quest) is a trip to New Zealand, then your baby steps (aka TO-DOs) could be to research airfares to New Zealand and start to save $x per week. If your Bullet Point (aka Quest) is to make a music video, then your baby steps (aka TO-DO) could be to research what you need to make the video, researching the costs of making the video, and researching fundraising websites such as kickstarter.com which will help you raise money to make the music video.

3. Now at least once a week:
   - <u>If you are using Quest Master®</u>, look at each Quest and each TO-DO and make sure you have added your Accomplishments for that week. Because Quest Master is portable in your phone, you will be able to on a daily basis enter your Accomplishments real time. For example, you will be entering notes and audio reminders as you think of them, taking photos and video real time, entering expenses as you incur them, income as you earn it, scheduling events, and adding contacts, etc. Quest Master automatically adds the date of each entry you make. Quest Master will become the one stop repository for your goal and your progress!

   - <u>If you are using this book's Journaling Pages</u>, at least once a week you should go to each Bullet Point's journaling page and check in. You will write down, on that journaling page, the date you are checking in, and in one quick line annotate what you did towards achieving your goal. For example, if you've done nothing (and that happens once in awhile), then your check in might read "nothing to report" or if you did baby steps, then your check in might read "researched kickstarter.com for fundraising" or it could be "signed up for a business plan writing class" or it could be "made reservations to attend a tradeshow."

If you're like me, the act of either using Quest Master or checking in and updating your Journaling Pages will become a satisfying, cozy, Zen-like thing to do.

I promise you, DOING is the main difference between a dream and achievement, and to my thinking, the saddest thing for me, for my personal ruler, is to NOT DO.

SUCCESS IS SOMETHING WE DESIGN FOR OURSELVES

INSPIRATION

For me, almost every one of my dreams has come true, and I attribute that success to setting goals and holding myself accountable for achieving them by journaling my progress. **Here are a few of the things I tell myself for inspiration** (you can find more of my sayings in my books *High Spirits!* and *Tempo – The Rhythm & Rhyme of the Artist*):

None of us can control what the universe brings us, but we can control our attitude and effort.

If at first you don't succeed, try, try, try, try, try, try, try, try again. Repeat as necessary.

Your job is to do your best, and let the universe take care of the rest.

Don't sweat what you can't control — but DO sweat — sweat equity — what you CAN control. You can control your effort, professionalism, diligence, integrity, and much more.

You are ultimately accountable for your own dreams.

- **GIVE YOURSELF PERMISSION**

- **DEFINE YOUR GOALS** – enter Quests into Quest Master or handwrite bullet points into Journaling Pages

- **DEFINE SOME STEPS** – enter TO-DOs into Quest Master or handwrite TO-DOs into Journaling Pages

- **DO!** – enter Accomplishments into Quest Master or handwrite updates into your Journaling Pages.

- **UPDATE YOUR JOURNALING PAGES OR QUEST MASTER REGULARLY!**

- **DO MORE!!! KEEP GOING!!!!**

Live – DO - Be Well! The Artimagination, Inc. team is rooting for you, and for your Success! Please share your successes at www.Quest.bz

We believe that Quest Master is the ideal tool to help you achieve your goals. To learn more about Quest Master and how to purchase it, please visit www.Quest.bz

Remember, you can be as high-tech or as low-tech as you want in tracking your progress and being accountable for your goals – the point is to do and to achieve! While we hope you decide Quest Master® Achievement app is right for you, an alternative to Quest Master is for you to use the following Journaling Pages – the rest is up to You!!!!

DEDICATION

This Book is Dedicated to all People who dare to dream.

SUCCESS IS SOMETHING WE DESIGN FOR OURSELVES

Journaling Pages

JOURNALING PAGES FOR BULLET POINT ONE HERE:

Write one of your bullet point goals here:

_____

Write down write at least two things you can start doing now towards achieving this bullet point.

_____

_____

_____

Check-in every week below and write down the date you are checking in, and in one quick line annotate what you did towards achieving your goal.

_____

_____

_____

_____

SUCCESS IS SOMETHING WE DESIGN FOR OURSELVES

SUCCESS IS SOMETHING WE DESIGN FOR OURSELVES

JOURNALING PAGES FOR BULLET POINT TWO HERE:

Write one of your bullet point goals here:

_____

Write down write at least two things you can start doing now towards achieving this bullet point.

_____

_____

_____

Check-in every week below and write down the date you are checking in, and in one quick line annotate what you did towards achieving your goal.

_____

_____

_____

SUCCESS IS SOMETHING WE DESIGN FOR OURSELVES

SUCCESS IS SOMETHING WE DESIGN FOR OURSELVES

JOURNALING PAGES FOR BULLET POINT THREE HERE:

Write one of your bullet point goals here:

_____

Write down write at least two things you can start doing now towards achieving this bullet point.

_____

_____

_____

Check-in every week below and write down the date you are checking in, and in one quick line annotate what you did towards achieving your goal.

_____

_____

_____

_____

SUCCESS IS SOMETHING WE DESIGN FOR OURSELVES

SUCCESS IS SOMETHING WE DESIGN FOR OURSELVES

JOURNALING PAGES FOR BULLET POINT FOUR HERE:

Write one of your bullet point goals here:

_____

Write down write at least two things you can start doing now towards achieving this bullet point.

_____

_____

_____

Check-in every week below and write down the date you are checking in, and in one quick line annotate what you did towards achieving your goal.

_____

_____

_____

SUCCESS IS SOMETHING WE DESIGN FOR OURSELVES

SUCCESS IS SOMETHING WE DESIGN FOR OURSELVES

JOURNALING PAGES FOR BULLET POINT FIVE HERE:

Write one of your bullet point goals here:

_____

Write down write at least two things you can start doing now towards achieving this bullet point.

_____

_____

_____

Check-in every week below and write down the date you are checking in, and in one quick line annotate what you did towards achieving your goal.

_____

_____

_____

_____

SUCCESS IS SOMETHING WE DESIGN FOR OURSELVES

SUCCESS IS SOMETHING WE DESIGN FOR OURSELVES

JOURNALING PAGES FOR BULLET POINT SIX HERE:

Write one of your bullet point goals here:

_____

Write down write at least two things you can start doing now towards achieving this bullet point.

_____

_____

_____

Check-in every week below and write down the date you are checking in, and in one quick line annotate what you did towards achieving your goal.

_____

_____

_____

_____

SUCCESS IS SOMETHING WE DESIGN FOR OURSELVES

SUCCESS IS SOMETHING WE DESIGN FOR OURSELVES

JOURNALING PAGES FOR BULLET POINT SEVEN HERE:

Write one of your bullet point goals here:

_____

Write down write at least two things you can start doing now towards achieving this bullet point.

_____

_____

_____

Check-in every week below and write down the date you are checking in, and in one quick line annotate what you did towards achieving your goal.

_____

_____

_____

_____

SUCCESS IS SOMETHING WE DESIGN FOR OURSELVES

SUCCESS IS SOMETHING WE DESIGN FOR OURSELVES

JOURNALING PAGES FOR BULLET POINT EIGHT HERE:

Write one of your bullet point goals here:

_____

Write down write at least two things you can start doing now towards achieving this bullet point.

_____

_____

_____

Check-in every week below and write down the date you are checking in, and in one quick line annotate what you did towards achieving your goal.

_____

_____

_____

_____

SUCCESS IS SOMETHING WE DESIGN FOR OURSELVES

SUCCESS IS SOMETHING WE DESIGN FOR OURSELVES

JOURNALING PAGES FOR BULLET POINT NINE HERE:

Write one of your bullet point goals here:

_____

Write down write at least two things you can start doing now towards achieving this bullet point.

_____

_____

_____

Check-in every week below and write down the date you are checking in, and in one quick line annotate what you did towards achieving your goal.

_____

_____

_____

SUCCESS IS SOMETHING WE DESIGN FOR OURSELVES

SUCCESS IS SOMETHING WE DESIGN FOR OURSELVES

JOURNALING PAGES FOR BULLET POINT TEN HERE:

Write one of your bullet point goals here:

_____

Write down write at least two things you can start doing now towards achieving this bullet point.

_____

_____

_____

Check-in every week below and write down the date you are checking in, and in one quick line annotate what you did towards achieving your goal.

_____

_____

_____

_____

SUCCESS IS SOMETHING WE DESIGN FOR OURSELVES

SUCCESS IS SOMETHING WE DESIGN FOR OURSELVES

SUCCESS IS SOMETHING WE DESIGN FOR OURSELVES

About Quest Master®

What makes Quest Master® Achievement Software unique is that it works for any type of goal, it allows you to track your progress towards each goal easily, and it allows you to input and view income, expenses, photos, audio, video, notes, contacts, and events both by goal and by type. In other words, at a glance you can see all the income, expenses, photos, audio, video, notes, contacts, and events associated with a particular goal of yours, or you can see all your notes together, all your income items together, etc.

Quest Master® achievement software tools are ideal for the entrepreneur, start-up business owner, artist, software programmer, photographer, writer, chef/recipe collector, hobbyist, or anyone seeking to achieve a dream. The patent pending Quest Master® software is provided to you by the Quest Master brand team at Artimagination, Inc. The Quest Master team actually used Quest Master® achievement tools to build Quest Master brand software! Please visit www.Quest.bz to learn more!

Here's how Quest Master® achievement tools work:

Using our Quest Master® app, you will write down a few words to describe a dream that you would really love to achieve. An example of a dream might be to write a cell phone app, paint a great painting, take an award winning photo of the Grand Canyon, achieve $100,000 in sales, publish your first novel, visit New Zealand, collect some great recipes, track your baseball cards or garage sale hobby, or to lose 20 pounds.

Whatever your dream, we call this dream a "Quest."

After you've identified your Quest, Quest Master® tools give you a 'magic button' to track your progress in achieving your Quest, using media (photos, video and audio), notes, scheduling, contacts, expenses, income, and more, all in one convenient place.

No more hunting all over your mobile device looking for that one picture, note or old calendar entry – now you can find everything relating to your Quest in one place – simply by using this Quest Master™ app! You can also use Quest Master™ software tools to organize and save recipes, photographs, videos, audio, to track income and expenses, organize your new house or car search, keep track of daily to-do's, and much more!

Why are Quest Master™ tools Different:

Only Quest Master™ tools have a single convenient  button!

With one cost-effective Quest Master® app, by simply using our unique 'Add Your Progress' button, you can:

• Track your progress and accomplishments, AND

• Access all your important related info in one convenient list for each Quest, AND

• Schedule events towards achieving your Quest, add photos/video/audio and notes for each Quest, identify key contacts for each Quest, and track your expenses and income relating to each Quest (very helpful at Tax Time!).

Quest Master® achievement tools are also the ultimate in flexibility – you don't need to be clairvoyant or spend hours planning for the Quest Master® app to work, and you don't need to create an exhaustive list of every step you'll need to take in the future to accomplish your dreams. **In fact, all you need to get started achieving your dream using Quest Master® tools is your dream and just one idea for a first step on the path towards your dream.**

Quest Master® brand achievement software is designed so that you can see and track all your notes, media, events, contacts, income and expenses for a particular Quest. For added flexibility, we know that sometimes you might wish to see all your media together (or all your notes, income, expenses, contacts or events), so we've arranged for you to be able to do that

SUCCESS IS SOMETHING WE DESIGN FOR OURSELVES

too, at the push of one button. That means you can also see, regardless of what Quest you are in, all your media, notes, events, contacts, income and expenses – very helpful!

Quest Master® brand software also has a unique color-coded icon format to help you classify your progress at a glance. For example, the Contacts icon is predominantly orange and when you view your progress you will see that each Quest Master® app Contact has an orange font associated with it. You can also see a color-coded list of your Events to show you at a glance the timing of Events. The full Quest Master® app Color Chart is available in our User Manual.

We believe that when you see how FUN and FULFILLING it is to see progress towards your dreams, and when you see how easy it is to track your progress, that you will accomplish many, many Quests with our Quest Master® app! We even used the Quest Master® achievement app to help us create the Quest Master® achievement app!

Quest Master® for Business

Here's how the Quest Master® Achievement app works:

Using our Quest Master® app, you will write down a few words to describe a goal that you would really love to achieve. An example of a goal might be to own your own business, to incorporate, to create a website for your business, to write your own cell phone app, to achieve $100,000 in sales, to manage client projects in connection with each client (equally great for plumbers and tradespeople as it is for managing sales or graphic design projects), to create a social media presence, to manage your yearly corporate filings, to manage your intellectual property (such as trademark, copyright, or patent) matters, to manage travel plans, to manage contacts and follow-ups from a tradeshow, to track business mileage, etc. In other words, the Quest Master® app is designed to work for virtually any goal you choose. Whatever your goal, we call this goal a "Quest."

After you've identified your Quest, Quest Master® Achievement gives you a 'magic button' – the 'Add Your Progress' button to track your progress in achieving your Quest, using media (photos, video and audio), notes, scheduling, contacts, expenses, income, and more, all in one convenient place.

Example: Let's say your goal is to start your own business. That becomes your Quest - 'Start my own Business.' Next you input one or two To-Dos that might get you started on the path to starting your own business. Important: All you need is one To-Do to get started - you don't need an exhaustive list and you don't need to do a lot of research to get a lot of use from this app. For our example of starting your own business, let's say that you have one To-Do that is "Research the Web" on what to do first. You do a Google search and find the Small Business Administration website at SBA.gov, so you can input your progress under the "Research the Web" To-Do in any of the following ways (choose whichever is most practical for you):

   - as a quick note (eg, "found SBA.gov") or
   - as a photo (take a screen capture of the SBA.gov page)
   - as an audio recording (record a quick reminder to yourself about SBA.gov being a great starting point)
   - as a contact (input the SBA.gov web address as a contact)

Once you input your SBA.gov info in any of the above ways, any time you look at your 'Start my own Business' Quest, you will see the SBA.gov info.

Let's say that after researching SBA.gov you decide to incorporate. You can manage that using the Quest Master® app as well, by creating a second To-Do called 'Incorporate.' As the incorporation process progresses, you can then use the Quest Master® app to record the incorporation fees as an expense, you can store your Articles of Incorporation and Statement of Information as a photo, you can store a hint to remember your login data for various websites, and you can record key dates in the Quest Master® app as events.

Once you input your SBA.gov info as above, any time you look at your 'Start my own Business' Quest, you will see the original SBA.gov info AND you will see the expenses incurred, the paperwork generated, and key dates.

Every time you enter a note, photo, audio, video, contact, event, expense or income item into your Quest Master® app, that in Quest Master lingo is called entering an "Accomplishment."

As your knowledge progresses over time, so will your list of Quests and your list of To-Dos - you might eventually have To-Dos for a resale certificate (aka Seller's Permit"), for intellectual

SUCCESS IS SOMETHING WE DESIGN FOR OURSELVES

property filings, and once your business is set up you might create an entirely new Quest for 'Making First $100,000 in Sales', etc. If you do have such a Quest for 'Making First $100,000 in Sales' then your To-Dos might include marketing efforts, website and social media development, trade shows and more, and any time a particular marketing effort results in an expense you can record that expense in the context of the specific marketing effort that incurred the expense. Similarly, any time a particular marketing effort results in a sale, you can record that sale as an income item in the context of the particular marketing effort that generated that sale. In this manner, at a glance you can see what marketing efforts are more effective than others.

What makes this Quest Master® app so powerful is that not only can you input data relating to your goals in a way that makes sense and evolves with your own speed of progress, but you will eliminate all that annoying hunting all over your mobile device looking for that one picture, note or old calendar entry – now you can find everything relating to your Quest in one place. Met someone at a tradeshow but can't remember their name? All you need to do is look at the Quest for that tradeshow. For those times that you want to see all your data together (such as all notes together, all income items together, all expense items together, etc)(as might be useful at tax time), the Quest Master® app enables you to do that as well, at the touch of an icon.

BEFORE USING THE QUEST MASTER® ACHIEVEMENT APP OR OUR WEBSITE, PLEASE SEE OUR PRIVACY POLICY and LEGAL CONDITIONS OF USE:
When you click on the Feedback/License icon in the Quest Master® app, then you will go to a menu screen with links to our Privacy Policy, Legal Conditions of Use, Feedback and About screens. You can also review **our Privacy Policy and Legal Conditions of Use on our website. It is very important that you carefully review our Legal Conditions of Use and Privacy Policy, as each is binding on you and you should not use Quest Master or our website if you do not agree to these legal terms and conditions.**

·WE WANT TO HEAR FROM YOU!

Have you finished a Quest and wish to share your success? Please visit our <u>Facebook page</u> or our <u>website chatroom</u> and share your success!

www.ingramcontent.com/pod-product-compliance
Lightning Source LLC
Chambersburg PA
CBHW081016040426
42444CB00014B/3235